This doodle book belongs to

Name:_____

Date:_____

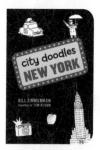  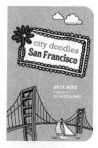

 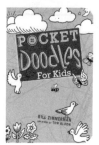 

Collect Them All!

Available at bookstores or
directly from Gibbs Smith

1.800.835.4993

www.pocketdoodles.com

city doodles
CHICAGO

ANNA M. LEWIS
DRAWINGS BY DANIEL CHAFFIN

GIBBS SMITH
TO ENRICH AND INSPIRE HUMANKIND

For my family—Robert, Emily, Hayden,
and Everett—who continually inspire me
with their humor and creativity.
—Anna

Manufactured in Altona, Manitoba, Canada
in June 2013 by Friesen

First Edition
17 16 15 14 13   5 4 3 2 1

Text © 2013 Anna M. Lewis
Illustrations © 2013 Daniel Chaffin

Published by
Gibbs Smith
P.O. Box 667
Layton, Utah 84041

1.800.835.4993 orders
www.gibbs-smith.com

Designed by Melissa Dymock and Renee Bond
Gibbs Smith books are printed on either recycled, 100%
post-consumer waste, FSC-certified papers or on paper
produced from sustainable PEFC-certified forest/
controlled wood source. Learn more at www.pefc.org.

ISBN: 978-1-4236-3479-9

Welcome!

You may have picked up this book because you are heading to or ending a trip to Chicago. You may live in or just love Chicago. In any case, though Chicago is nicknamed the Second City, you will find that it is a city of many firsts.

While exploring this creative and innovative city through our book, we hope you find a way to spark some doodle talents and see your drawings fly off the page.

Happy Doodling!

Anna and Daniel

Visit the Skydeck on top of Willis Tower for a bird's-eye view of the Chicago area. Draw the buildings below.

What sights can you see in the fifty-mile view? Add them to the drawing.

Willis Tower, at 108 stories, is the second-tallest building in the United States. Finish drawing the windows.

Design your own skyscraper in the clouds.

For another perspective, float through
downtown on a Chicago River tour.
Doodle people on a cruise boat.

Add the buildings and bridges that
you pass. If it's St. Patrick's Day,
color the river green.

Go for a spin on Lake Michigan in a sailboat. Chicago has the largest harbor system in the United States with over six thousand boat slips. Add sails to the boat.

Doodle other boats in the lake.

Take the L through the city. Chicago's elevated train has been a major source of transit around Chicago for over one hundred years. Doodle people on their way to work.

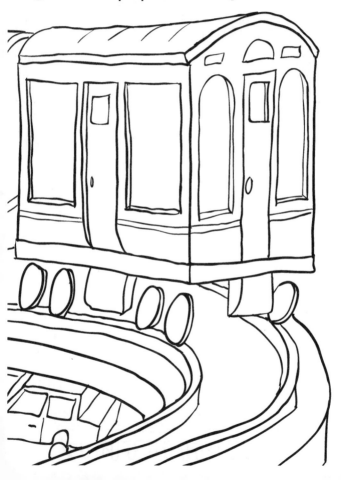

The L goes around Chicago's main business area. Why is it called the "Loop"? Draw the streets inside it.

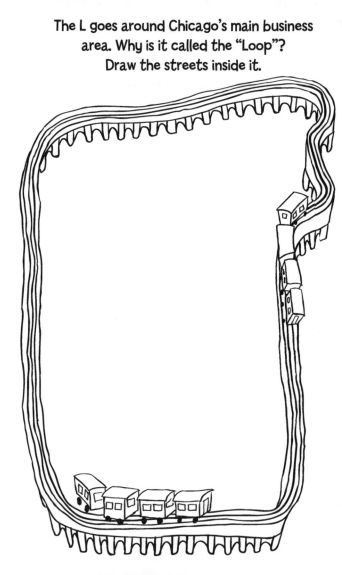

Within the Loop, sitting next to the lake, is Grant Park, known as "Chicago's front yard." Covering 319 acres, there's a lot that you can do. Draw a street performer in the park.

Doodle people playing in the park.

Within Grant Park is the gigantic Buckingham Fountain, known as "Chicago's front door." It's one of the world's largest fountains. Finish doodling the water spraying and add details to the fountain.

Surrounding the fountain are four
seahorses that represent the four
states that border the lake: Illinois,
Wisconsin, Michigan, and Indiana.
Doodle fins and scales on the seahorse.

A few steps away is the Art Institute of Chicago, built in 1893. Dress up one of the two lions that stand guard outside the front door.

Inside, you will find the world-famous
painting *American Gothic* by Grant Wood.
Add your face and a family
member to the painting.

You can't miss George Seurat's *A Sunday Afternoon on the Island of La Grande Jette*. It's seven feet tall and ten feet wide. Add some details to this scene on the Seine River in Paris.

Add people looking at the painting in the museum. What are they saying about this painting made of dots?

Explore the new Modern Wing built
in 2009. Add shapes to an Alexander
Calder mobile hanging from the ceiling.

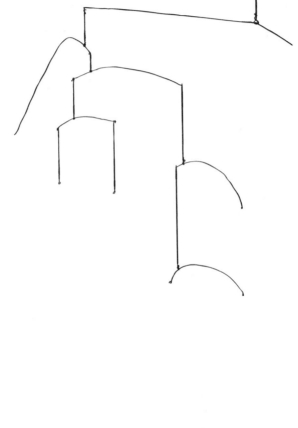

Design a tiny room from the Thorne Miniature Rooms, found on the lower level.

Millennium Park is the newest addition to Grant Park. At over thirty feet high and sixty-six feet wide, "The Bean" stands alone. The skyline is reflected in the mirrored surface. Draw your distorted reflection.

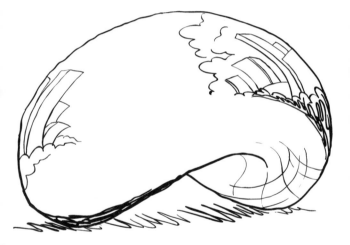

This sculpture was created by artist Anish Kapoor and titled *Cloud Gate*. Why do you think he called it that?

Show everyone taking pictures
and making faces.

See a show or concert at the Jay Pritzker
Pavilion designed by architect Frank Gehry.
A piece of art, the 120-foot-high
stage looks like stainless steel ribbons.
Add more ribbons to the stage.

Sketch the people in the audience.

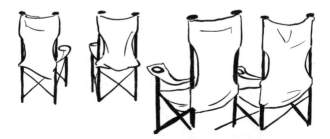

Look up as you walk through the front doors of the Field Museum and be greeted by Sue, a thirteen-foot-high and forty-two-foot-long Tyrannosaurus Rex. Finish drawing in some of Sue's bones.

What would Sue say to you? Add sharp teeth to Sue's mouth.

Wander into the Egyptian tomb
and see the twenty-three mummies.
Create your own mummy doodle.

Show off some sparkly rocks from the Halls of Gems and Jades.

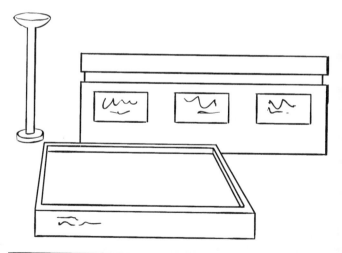

Dive into the Shedd Aquarium.
Fill in the tank with some of the
25,000 different types of fish.

Doodle the sea life in the Caribbean Reef.

Watch the animals perform at the aquatic show. Can you doodle the dolphins flying and the beluga whales dancing?

Add some kids enjoying the show.
Do they get splashed?

Gaze into the stars at the Adler Planetarium—the first planetarium in the U.S. Add lots and lots of stars to the domed ceiling in the Grainger Sky Theater.

Doodle everyone looking up at the galaxies.

Ready for some fun? Race over to Navy Pier, known as "Chicago's lakefront playground." With over nine million visitors a year, it's the Midwest's number one tourist destination. On the pier, what's the street performer juggling? Doodle a few tourists watching.

Draw the unicycle that the clown is riding.

Take a ride on the fifteen-story-tall Ferris wheel, designed after the first Ferris wheel at Chicago's 1893 World's Columbian Exposition. Doodle people in the gondolas waving and enjoying the lake view.

If there are forty gondolas and six people can sit in each one, how many people can ride on the Ferris wheel at a time?

Finish the hot air balloon
floating over the lake.

Go inside and check out the Chicago Children's Museum. Show all the kids climbing, splashing, and exploring.

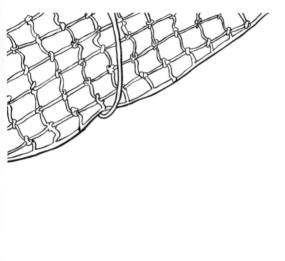

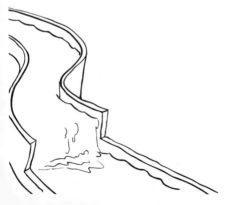

In the Skyline exhibit, what would
you build a skyscraper with?

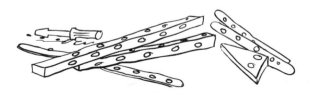

Heading north along seven miles of the lakeshore is the 1,208-acre Lincoln Park, named after Abraham Lincoln. With over twenty million visitors each year, it's the second-most visited park in the United States. What is this Lincoln statue thinking?

There are replicas of this famous statue
by Augustus Saint-Gaudens around
the world. Can you doodle a copy?

Say hello to the park's many statues.
Benjamin Franklin, Alexander Hamilton,
and William Shakespeare are just a few.
What are they saying to each other?

Draw a statue of someone you admire.

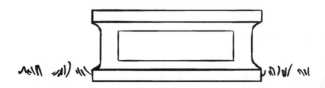

Surprised to see a zoo in the middle of a city? The Lincoln Park Zoo is a free 35-acre home to over 1,250 animals. Make a list of all the animals you might see.

Lincoln Park Animals

Draw the gorillas and chimpanzees swinging from the trees in the Regenstein Center for African Apes.

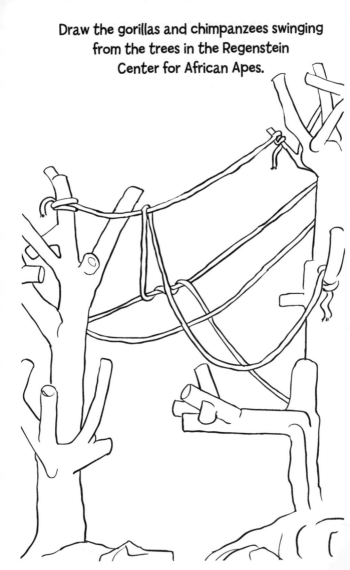

Founded in 1868, the Lincoln Park Zoo is one of the oldest in the U.S. The first residents at the zoo were two swans given as gifts. Draw swans swimming in the pond.

In 1930, when an orphaned baby gorilla named Bushman came to the zoo, he became an instant celebrity.
Doodle a baby gorilla.

All aboard the LPZoo Express Train.
Draw some kids having fun riding the train.

Stop by the Kovler Sea Lion Pool, built in 1879, and watch the gray seals being fed. Show all the visitors lined up along the fence to watch the show.

Draw some whiskers on this cute baby seal.

Built between 1890 and 1895, the Lincoln Park Conservatory shows exotic plants from around the world. Draw more ferns, palms, and orchids in this planter.

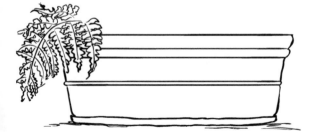

Plant some beautiful flowers
in front of the conservatory.

Get in touch with nature at the North Pond Nature Sanctuary. This habitat for wildlife is built around a ten-acre pond. Watch the birds catch fish. Draw what this heron caught in his mouth.

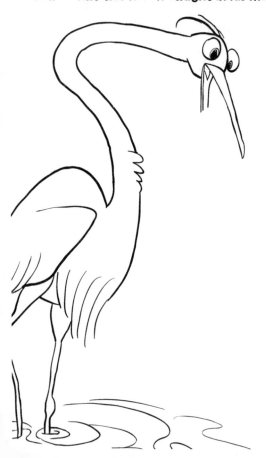

Doodle some of the 150 species of native Illinois plants that grow around the pond.

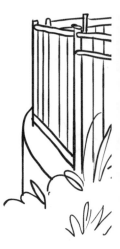

Grab your binoculars! Check off what you saw or could see. Include some of the two hundred birds that you may see.

Native Illinois Wildlife

- ☐ Red fox
- ☐ Coyote
- ☐ Opossum
- ☐ Raccoon
- ☐ Butterfly
- ☐ Dragonfly
- ☐ Frog
- ☐ Turtle
- ☐ Great Blue Heron
- ☐ Wood Ducks

Draw some of these animals.

Getting hungry? Grab a
Chicago-Style Hot Dog.

Recipe:

Hot Dog	Tomatoes
Poppy seed Bun	Pickle
Mustard	Peppers
Relish	Dash of Celery Salt
Onions	

Draw some wild things you
might put on a hot dog.

Snack on some Chicago-Style Popcorn.

Recipe:

Cheesy popcorn + Caramel popcorn

Can you think of some other salty and sweet combinations from Chicago?

Take me out to a ball game? Let's head to the north side for a Chicago Cubs game at Wrigley Field. Write the name of your favorite baseball team on the marquee at the entrance to the field.

Draw the people entering.

What's Chicago's other baseball team?
Hint: They come up to bat later in this book.

Finish drawing the famous ivy at the outfield wall.

Add the bases and some of the players on the field. Play ball!

Chicago's name may have come from the Potawatomi Indian name for wild onion—*checagou*. Draw the wild onion growing along the riverbank.

Some say the name came from the
Native American name for striped skunk.
Sketch a skunk on the riverbank.

John-Baptiste Point de Sable, manager of a trading post, was the first official resident of Chicago. Draw the log cabin that he built on the banks of the Chicago River.

What items do you think he sold?

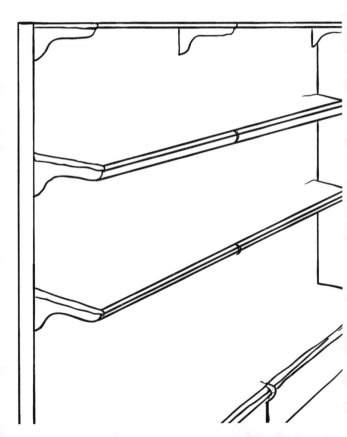

Dearborn was built in 1803 and became the westernmost U.S. military outpost.
Draw a military fort.

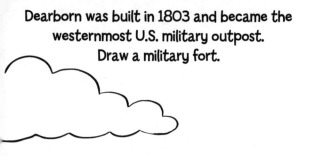

In 1833, Chippewa, Ottawa, and Potawatomi tribes signed a treaty selling five million acres of land, making Chicago officially a town. Draw Native Americans in canoes on Lake Michigan.

By 1870, Chicago grew very quickly into a major city with nearly 300,000 people. Finish drawing a street lined with two-story wooden houses.

Chicago's first nickname was "mud hole of the prairie." The soggy streets were covered with wood planks. Add details to the horse-drawn carriage on the wooden street.

In May of 1871, the Chicago White Stockings became the city's first professional baseball team. Add a bat and ball to this player's baseball card.

The White Stockings eventually changed their name to the Chicago Cubs. Finish drawing this Cub player's baseball card.

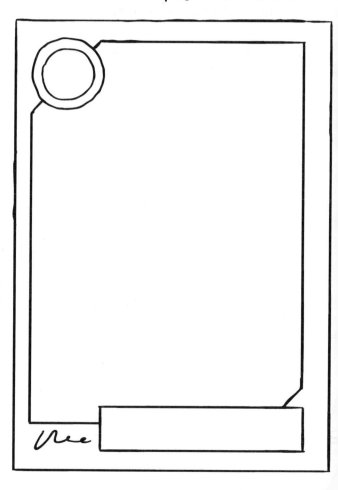

In October 1871, Chicago was in the middle of a severe drought. They had one of the nation's first fire departments, but the fire that broke out in the O'Leary barn quickly grew out of control. Add details to this horse-drawn fire engine.

When the Great Fire ended, it destroyed an area four miles wide by almost a mile long. Write some headlines for the newspaper this paperboy is holding.

What do you think he is yelling to sell
papers to the Chicago residents when
one-third of the population was homeless?

To sell more papers, a reporter made up a story that Mrs. O'Leary's cow kicked a lamp and started the fire. The gossip exploded and soon everyone thought the story was true. Can you think of other ways that the fire might have started?

Cows became an unofficial symbol of the city. In 1999, Chicago hosted "Cows On Parade." Three hundred life-size cow statues decorated by local artists were displayed all over town. Decorate some of these cows and give them unique names.

On the 126th anniversary of the Great Fire, Chicago's new Major League Soccer team was named the Chicago Fire. Decorate the Chicago Fire team ball.

Draw more soccer players
racing to get the ball.

After the fire, Chicago quickly made plans to rebuild the city and attracted architects and engineers from around the world. With the growing population, land prices rose and designers had nowhere to go but up.

In 1882, Daniel Burnham and John Root designed the first building named "skyscraper"—the ten-story (130-foot) Montauk Building. Design some stone buildings.

The first "modern skyscraper" was built in 1884 by William Le Baron Jenney. The Home Insurance Building, at ten stories (138 feet), was the first building with a structural steel frame. Build a skyscraper using a steel frame.

The Montauk and the Home Insurance Buildings were both ten stories high. Which one is taller?

In 1893, Chicago hosted the World's Columbian Exposition. Entertaining and educating 27 million visitors, the fair introduced many new ideas to the world. Finish adding lights and details to the Electricity Building.

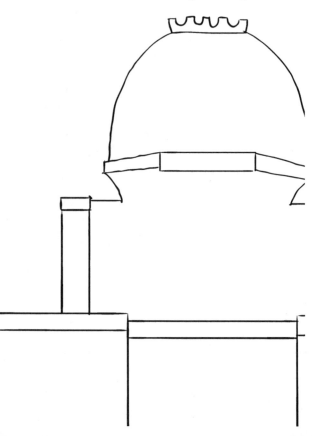

The U.S. population at this time was close to 70 million, so approximately what percentage of the U.S. attended the fair? Draw some faces on these fairgoers.

Visitors rode in the first Ferris wheel. At 264 feet high with 36 cars, the world had never seen such an attraction. Finish drawing the cars and the remaining steel structure.

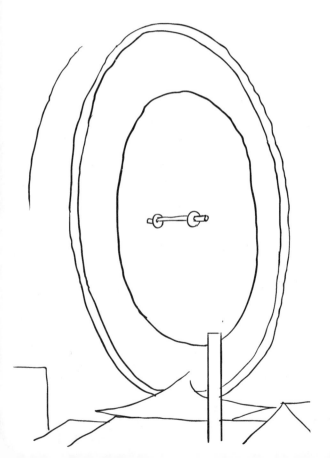

What do you think the people are saying?

When a visitor tried a new food,
candied popcorn and peanuts, he
exclaimed, "Cracker Jack!" Doodle more
of this snack in the visitor's hands.

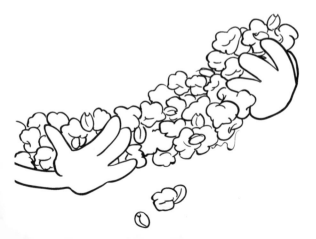

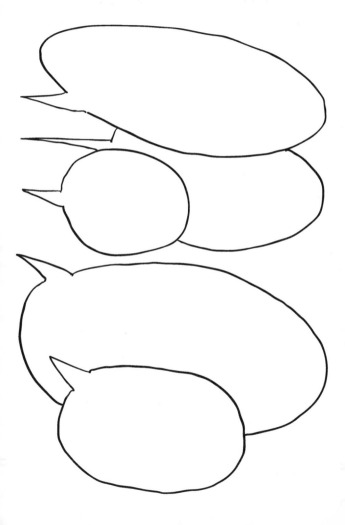

William Wrigley Jr. presented Juicy
Fruit gum. Design a gum wrapper.

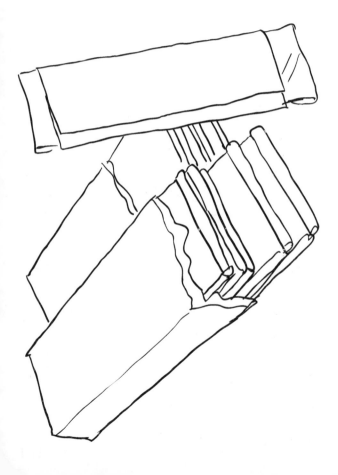

Hot dog! Putting a sausage on a bun became the simple solution for visitors wanting to eat and walk around the fair. Doodle hot dogs for all these fairgoers.

One of the architects of the 1893 World's Fair was Louis Sullivan, who was called "the father of modernism." One of many Chicago landmarks he built is the Carson, Pirie, Scott and Company Building. Add more windows using perspective.

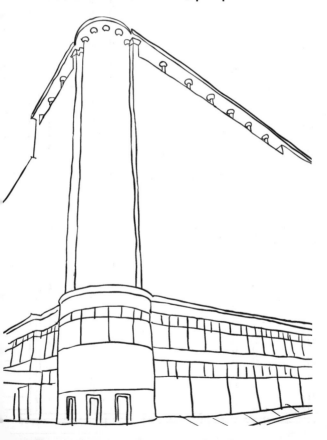

"Chicago windows" allowed more light and clean air into buildings. Give this window some curtains and decorations.

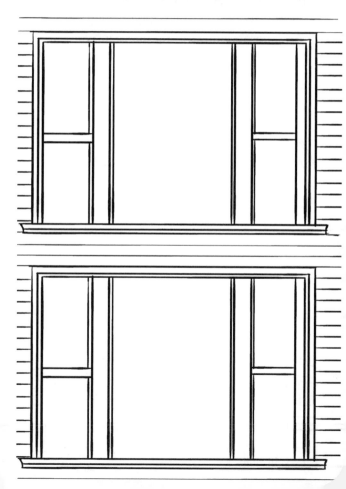

Architect Frank Lloyd Wright left Sullivan's
office and designed houses in the Oak
Park suburb of Chicago. His Prairie style
used horizontal lines and flat roofs.
Add more long shapes to this house.

Add trees and plants to fit the house into the landscape.

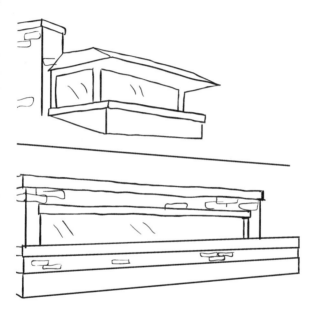

**Frank Lloyd Wright designed
the entire house, inside and out.
Create a stained glass window.**

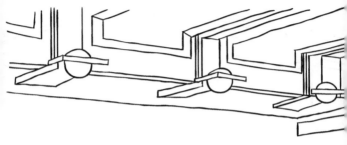

Build a chair and table using long and basic shapes.

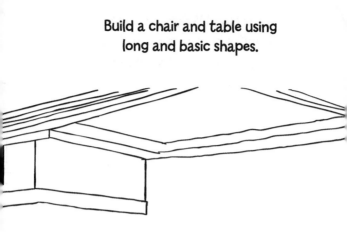

Frank Lloyd Wright changed American home design. He has been called "the greatest architect of all time." Design your dream house.

Make a list of what elements you need for your perfect house.

Take an airplane to Chicago. O'Hare Airport is one of the busiest in the world with over 64 million passengers a year. Draw the planes arriving and departing on the seven runways.

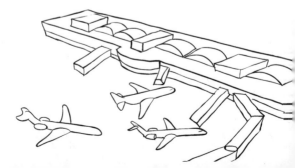

The airport is named after Edward O'Hare,
the U.S. Navy's first flying ace and
Medal of Honor recipient in World War II.
Draw the control towers.

Midway Airport was Chicago's first municipal airport. By 1929, it was the busiest in the world. Finish the details and add a pilot to this plane from the 1920s.

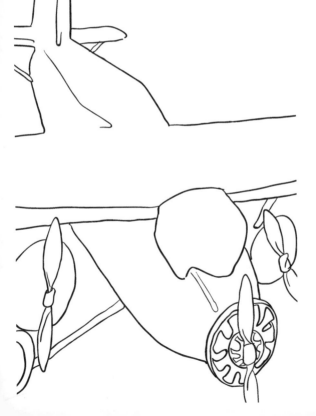

Give your plane a name.

Drive by car. Famous Route 66 started in front of the Art Institute on Michigan Avenue and ended in Los Angeles. Draw the path following the cities on the map.

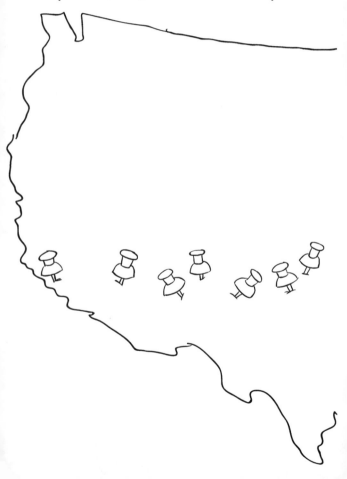

Decorate the map with sights you would find on your trip.

Take the Amtrak train. Relax in one of the fifty trains that arrive and depart each day. Add passengers on the train looking out the windows.

Sail a boat to Chicago Harbor. Add sails and a flag to this sailboat on Lake Michigan.

Add waves from the wind. Chicago is not the windiest city in the U.S. Here's how other cities compare in average wind speed:

Milton, MA: 15.4 mph

Boston, MA: 12.4 mph

Chicago, IL: 10.3 mph

New York City, NY: 9.3 mph

Los Angeles, CA: 7.5 mph

In July, the Race to Mackinac attracts yachts from around the world to Chicago. Started in 1898 and running 333 miles across Lake Michigan, the event is the longest and oldest annual freshwater sailing race in the world. Doodle more yachts of all sorts and sizes racing through the waves.

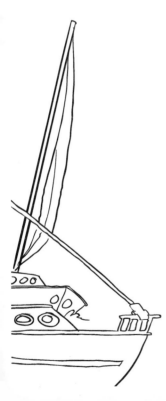

Chicago's nickname the "Windy City" refers to the boastful early city leaders, loudly proclaiming Chicago's greatness.

Add more things that the men are saying to each other.

Why is Chicago's other nickname "Second City"?

1. For many years, Chicago was second in size to New York City. Now, it is the third largest city in the U.S.

2. Chicago was able to rebuild itself after the Great Fire.

What cities do you think are next in population on the 2011 U.S. Census?

1. New York City: 8,244,910

2. Los Angeles: 3,819,702

3. Chicago: 2,707,120

4. _____

5. _____

6. _____

7. _____

8. _____

9. _____

10. _____

Label the names of the top ten cities in the U.S. on this map.

Chicago has many other nicknames. Draw
Chicagoans next to these greetings.

Give them a Cubs or White Sox hat
and a Bears t-shirt. Chicagoans
are very proud of their teams.

Chicago is a toy and game capital. Many toy companies are located here. Draw a Radio Flyer wagon.

Design a new Ty Beanie Baby.

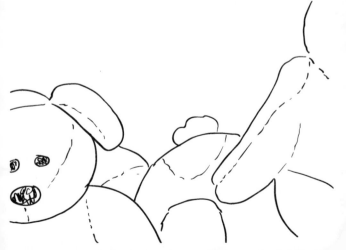

Inventors created some iconic games and toys here. Doodle the Operation game.

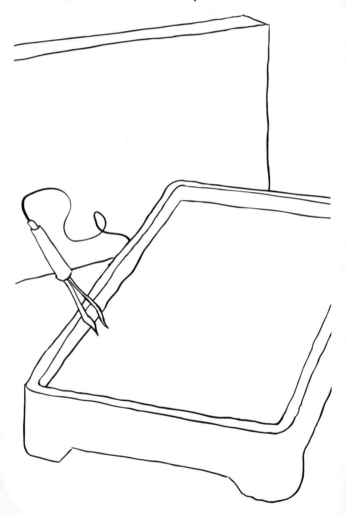

Make a Lite-Brite design.

John Lloyd Wright, son of architect
Frank Lloyd Wright, created Lincoln Logs.
Create a building using Lincoln Logs.

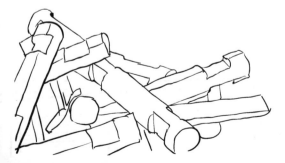

Invent a new toy or game idea.

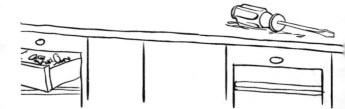

Chicago is a candy capital. Millions of
Tootsie Rolls are made here each day.
Add more Tootsie Rolls to the candy jar.

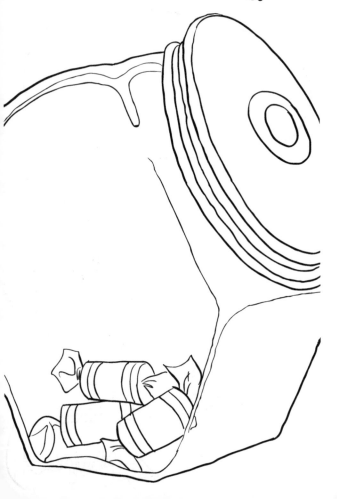

What's your favorite flavor Tootsie Pop? Give this kid a Tootsie Pop.

Snickers, the top candy bar, is made here.
There are about sixteen peanuts
per bar. Add them to this bar.

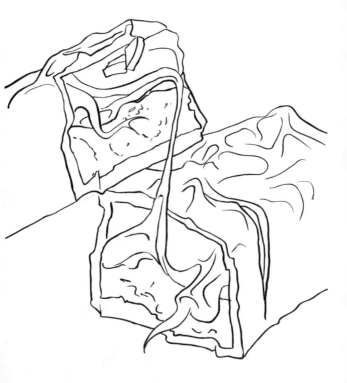

Design your own candy bar. What's your recipe? Give it a cool name.

Jelly Belly jelly beans are also made
in Chicago. Add colors and designs
to the beans in the candy jar.
How many beans do you count?

Create your own wild Jelly Belly flavor. Give it a funny name.

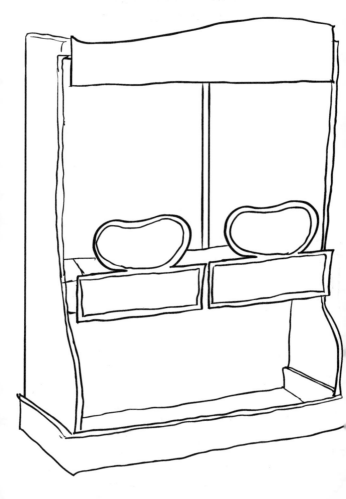

Brach's Confections was started in
Chicago in 1904. Write messages
on these Conversation Hearts.

Brach's Candy Corn is the best
selling in the world. Add more candy
corn to this Halloween scene.

"State Street, that great street."

Meeting at the Great Clocks in front of Macy's is a Chicago tradition. Place hands on the clocks.

Show friends greeting each other.

"Sentinels of State Street."

Macy's on State Street is the world's second largest department store. And, while the building was formerly Marshall Fields, now Macy's, it has the honor of being the first department store to have holiday windows. Add details to this holiday window.

Design your own store window.

Sit down to have tea in Macy's Walnut Room, the first department store tearoom. Draw ladies enjoying their lunch at the table.

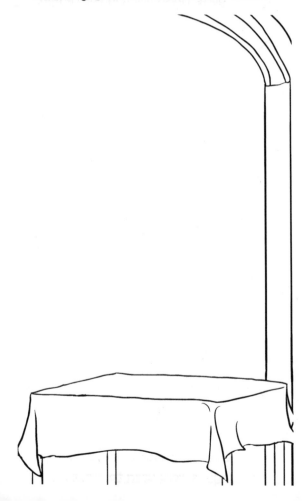

Look up and see the first and largest ceiling designed with Tiffany favrile glass. Finish filling in the design.

Over 1.6 million pieces of favrile glass were used to create it.

Go across the street to Daley Plaza and see
The Picasso, a Chicago landmark since 1967.
Draw people looking at the fifty-foot
sculpture. What do you think it is?

Create your own sculpture out of steel. Give your piece a name.

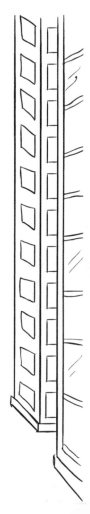

Walk by the ABC 7 News State Street studio at the right time and watch filming. Maybe you'll be on TV.

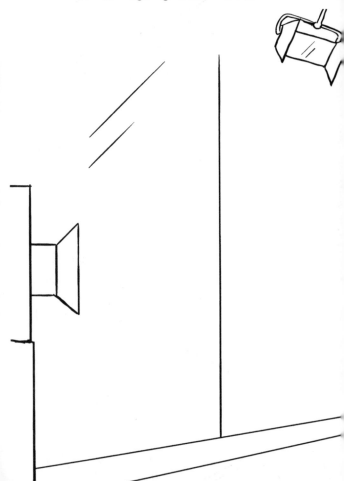

Add all the people looking in the
window at the newscasters.

At six stories high, the Chicago Theatre sign
and marquee stand out on State Street.
Finish adding lights to the sign.

When the theater opened in 1921, it was called the "Wonder Theater of the World." Add your favorite entertainer's name to the marquee.

The Harold Washington Library Center is the largest public library building in the world. Owl figures sit in seven forty-foot-tall aluminum sculptures around the rooftop. Draw an owl in the middle of the sculpture.

Design a fancy rooftop. Add
a gargoyle or two.

Go inside the library and look for
your favorite book. Add the title
and author to the bookshelf.

What do these books already on
the shelf have in common?

THE SUN ALSO RISES

ERNEST
HEMINGWAY

Tarzan of the Apes

Edgar Rice
Burroughs

The Giving Tree

SHEL
SILVERSTEIN

Answer: They were all written
by Chicago authors.

Add a book with your name as
author. Give that book a title.

Shop until you drop on the Magnificent Mile. Thirteen blocks along Michigan Avenue are home to over 400 exclusive world-class stores. Give these shoppers some bags.

The Magnificent Mile runs between Chicago River and The Drake Hotel. This distance is actually eight-tenths (or .8) of a mile. If a mile is 5,280 feet long, how many feet long is the Magnificent Mile?

Answer: 4,224 feet.

The Magnificent Mile Lights Festival is the nation's largest evening holiday celebration. Draw a float in the parade.

The Chicago Water Tower is a symbol of the city—gaining fame by being one of the only public structures left standing after the Great Fire. Finish adding details to this castle-like building.

White Castle restaurants were
built to look like the Water Tower.
Design your own castle.

The tall building next door is Water Tower Place. At seventy-four stories, it's the ninth-tallest building in Chicago. Check out the vertical mall inside. Doodle all the smartly dressed shoppers on the escalator.

The mall has eight stories of stores, restaurants and entertainment. Design stylish signs for your favorite stores.

Head up to the restaurant on the ninety-fifth floor of the John Hancock Center for one of the best views of the city. Finish adding the x-bracing design on the building.

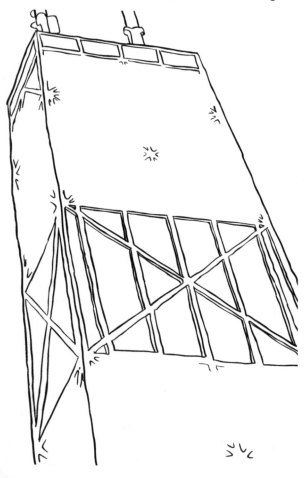

Draw the view these people
see out their window.

The John Hancock Center is one hundred stories tall, making it number four in Chicago and number seven in the U.S. On the forty-fourth floor is America's highest indoor swimming pool. Draw a pool for this guy making a cannonball.

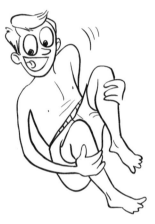

The building's elevator can travel up to 20.5 miles per hour. Draw some strangers in an elevator.

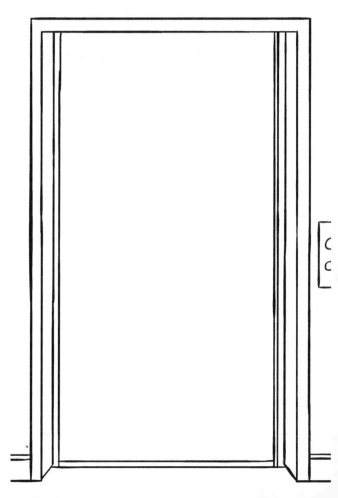

The Magnificent Mile begins at The
Drake Hotel, a landmark since 1920.
Finish drawing all the windows.

Draw taxis dropping off guests.
Celebrities and international
dignitaries stay at The Drake.

Can you see the two circular buildings by the river? That's Marina City. Draw two sixty-five-story buildings that look like corncobs.

Marina City is the home to the House of Blues. Draw your favorite singer performing on stage.

Head down Chicago Avenue to the Museum of Contemporary Art, one of the nation's largest museums for current art. Check out Claes Oldenburg's ten-foot-wide *Sculpture in the Form of a Fried Egg*. Draw a huge piece of toast to go with it.

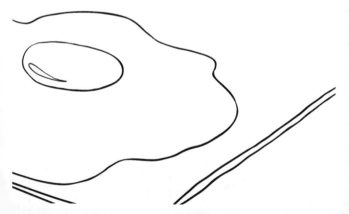

Design a pop art sculpture of an
object you use every day.

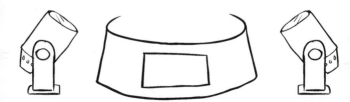

Along the Chicago River, look up to see Trump Tower. It was named after billionaire real estate developer Donald Trump, and at ninety-two stories it's the third-tallest building in the U.S. Add a few boats floating by on the river.

The Spa at Trump and the tower's hotel rooms are some of the finest in the world. Draw a lavish hotel suite.

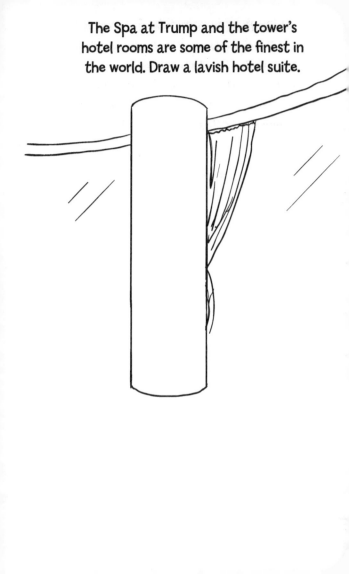

Have a laugh at Second City. For over fifty years, the comedy club has made us chuckle. Some famous comedians who started here are John Belushi, Stephen Colbert, Bill Murray, and Tina Fey. Draw some improv actors performing a comedy sketch.

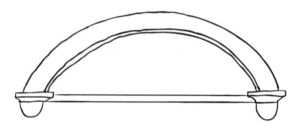

Give them more funny lines.

Chicago is home to the world-famous Joffrey Ballet—called "America's Company of Firsts." Add ballerinas with tutus performing on stage.

Draw people enjoying a holiday performance of *Nutcracker*.

What's that wavy building? That's the Aqua—at 859 feet it's the tallest building in the world designed by a woman. Draw a wavy skyscraper.

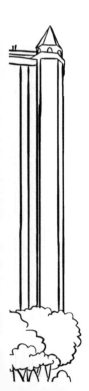

One of Chicago's newest landmarks, the Aqua incorporates many eco-friendly/green features. Add a garden to your wavy skyscraper design.

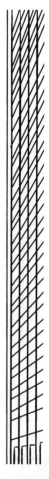

See a play at the Cadillac Palace Theatre. Built in 1926, Broadway shows often play here after leaving New York City. Draw the rows of people watching from the balcony.

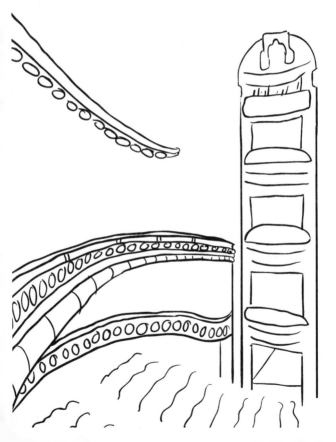

Draw a scene from your favorite
Broadway show on the stage.

In the Federal Plaza stands a fifty-four-foot steel sculpture named *Flamingo*. Created by Alexander Calder in 1974, it looks like a big red spider. Draw some of the people walking through the sculpture.

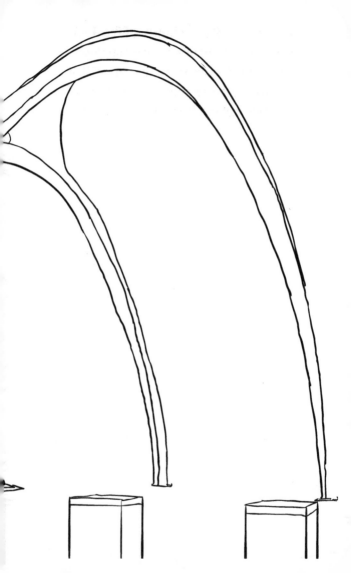

In 1978, the city council approved the
Percent-for-Art Ordinance, which requires
1.33 percent of the construction cost for
a building to be used on public artwork.
Add art to this new building.

Two hundred cities around the country
have adopted similar programs.
Create a sculpture to go with your art.

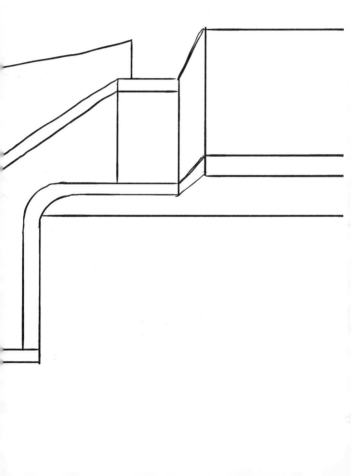

In mid-August, see the Chicago Air and Water Show. Doodle the U.S. Navy Blue Angels jetting through the skyscrapers.

Chicago has the oldest and largest free air and water show in the U.S. Add three more U.S. Air Force Thunderbird jets to this formation. Give them all vapor trails.

The building with the slanted roof that looks like it was chopped off is the Crain Communications Building. Add the diamond shape to the building.

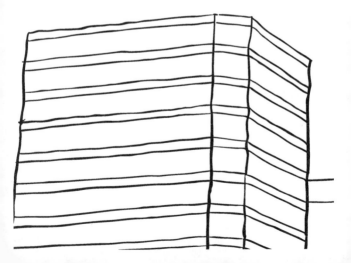

Lights on the roof sometimes spell out "Go Bears" or "Go Sox." Write something in lights on the slanted roof.

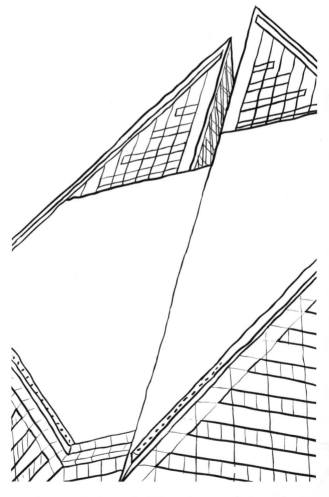

Are you ready for some football?
During the season, stop by Soldier
Field for a game. Add the missing yard
lines and yardages to this field.

Draw a Chicago Bears quarterback.
Give him a ball to toss to the receiver.

During the winter, grab some ice skates for some cold weather fun. Some popular rinks are McCormick Tribune Ice Rink at Millennium Park and Daley Bicentennial Plaza at Grant Park. Add more people enjoying the ice.

Look for ice sculptures.
Doodle an ice carving.

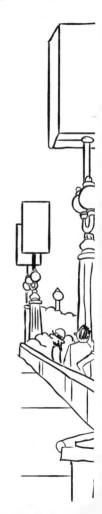

Watch the Chicago Bulls play a game of hoops at the United Center. Draw four more teammates for this center.

Give this player a ball for his slam dunk.

Want to grab a pizza—Chicago-style?
Deep-dish pizza was invented at
Pizzeria Uno in 1943. Add your favorite
toppings to this pizza slice.

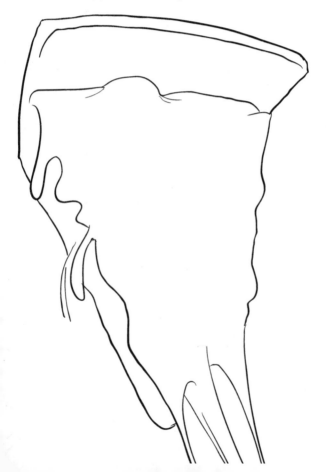

Give this guy a big slice of pizza.

Goal! Check out a Chicago Blackhawks hockey game at the United Center. Draw the net that his goalie is guarding. Give him a hockey stick.

Draw the Stanley Cup. Engrave your favorite NHL team's name on it.

Ready for a wild time? Head to the Brookfield Zoo. When it opened in 1934, the zoo was one of the first to use moats and ditches instead of cages. Draw a tiger on the rock above the moat.

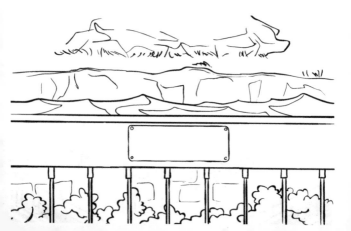

The Roosevelt Fountain, a zoo landmark, sits in the middle of the park. Add the forty-foot fountain spray in the center.

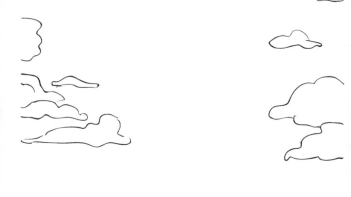

Su Lin, the first giant panda to be
exhibited in the U.S., made his home
at the zoo in 1937. Draw a panda
in these bamboo branches.

Draw Ziggy, a bull elephant, one of
the original stars of the zoo.

Add children taking a ride in this wagon.

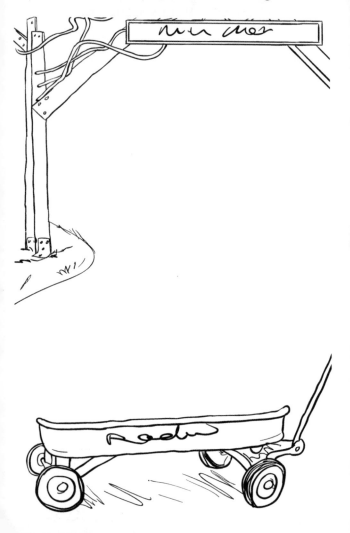

Doodle more kangaroos playing in the
Australia House. Add a baby joey.

Head over to the Seven Seas Dolphinarium
and watch the bottlenose dolphins perform.
Draw some dolphins putting on a show.

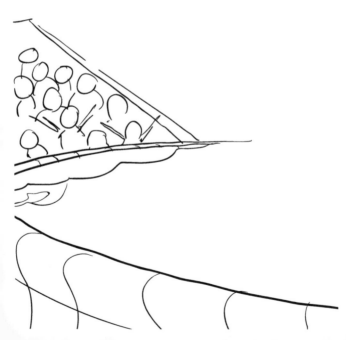

Hand the dolphin trainer a fish treat to reward the performers.

Play ball! Head to the south side for a
White Sox baseball game. Adopting the
name the Cubs abandoned, they became
a team in 1900. Total up the runs scored.

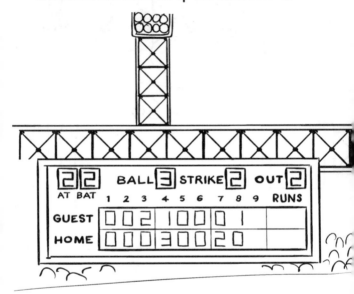

Add your favorite team's name to the
board. Draw some more players on the field.

White Sox
vs.

Give Southpaw, the White Sox
mascot, a baseball cap and a bat.

Write a chant so Southpaw can cheer on the players. Can you answer his questions?

Why am I named Southpaw?

Am I an alligator or a frog?

Answers: I'm a left-handed pitcher from the South Side. I'm just a green guy who loves the White Sox.

The Museum of Science and Industry opened in 1933 in The Palace of Fine Arts building used for the 1893 World Fair. Finish adding architectural details to this beautiful building.

Over 35,000 artifacts and fourteen acres of hands-on exhibits make this one of the largest science museums in the world. The Coal Mine was one of the first exhibits. Give this miner a coal bucket, hardhat and axe.

Draw some of the rooms in Colleen Moore's Fairy Castle.

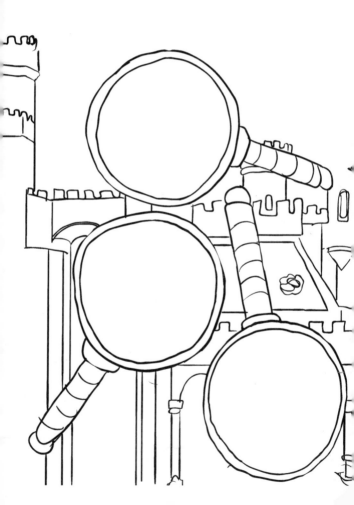

Take a tour of U-505, the only
German submarine in the U.S.
Draw an American flag on the pole.

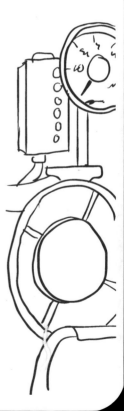
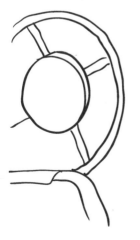

In the ToyMaker 3000 exhibit see how a toy top is manufactured. Create another robot arm in the assembly line.

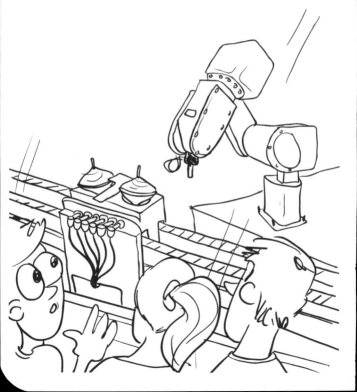

Add a design to this toy top.

The Great Train Story is a 3,500-square-foot model railroad showing the journey from Chicago to Seattle. Build a town around the railroad tracks.

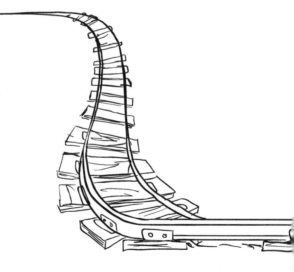

There are more than twenty trains running
in this exhibit. Add trains to the tracks.

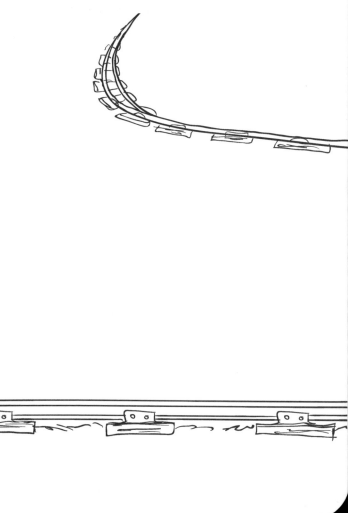

The Chicago Marathon is one of the five World Marathon Majors. There are spots for 45,000 runners. Add more runners.

Draw the winner running through the finish line. The Marathon starts and ends at Grant Park. How many miles is a marathon race?

Like books? In June, Printers Row Lit Fest is the largest free outdoor literary event in the Midwest. Show all the people under the publisher tents looking at books.

Draw an author or illustrator
sitting at a table.

When you write a book and have a book
signing, how will you sign your name?

Started in 1901, the Chicago Auto
Show is the largest in the U.S.
Doodle your dream car.

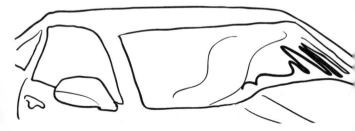

Draw all the people admiring your car.

Here's a list of Chicago's skyscrapers. Circle the buildings that we've visited in this book.

1.	Willis Tower	1,451 ft.	2nd Tallest in the U.S.
2.	Trump International Hotel and Tower	1,389 ft.	3rd Tallest in the U.S.
3.	Aon Center	1,136 ft.	6th Tallest in the U.S.
4.	John Hancock Center	1,127 ft.	7th Tallest in the U.S.
5.	Franklin Center North Tower	1,007 ft.	12th Tallest in the U.S.
6.	Two Prudential Plaza	995 ft.	14th Tallest in the U.S.
7.	311 South Wacker Dr.	961 ft.	17th Tallest in the U.S.
8.	900 North Michigan	871 ft.	
9.	Water Tower Place	859 ft.	
10.	Aqua	859 ft.	

Can you pick out the buildings
on the skyline? Label them.

In May 2013, One World Trade Center became
the tallest building in the U.S. by adding its
spire. As taller buildings are created, the
rankings of these skyscrapers may change,
though their history and legacy live on.

At the end of your day, enjoy the nighttime view of the city. Create a fireworks show above the skyline.

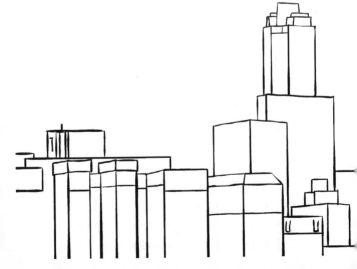

Add lights to the buildings.

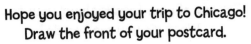

Hope you enjoyed your trip to Chicago!
Draw the front of your postcard.

Tell one of your friends about your trip.
What did you see and do?

Make a list of all the unique things
about Chicago that you have learned.
We already started the list for you.

Things that make Chicago great:

1. Buckingham Fountain—one of the world's largest

2. The Race to Mackinaw
   —the longest annual freshwater sailing race in the world

3. Toy and Game Capital